Table For Two

Table For Two

GUIDE FOR SENIOR'S DATING

LUCY MORGAN WALLER

To order additional copies of this book, contact:
Xlibris Corporation
1-888-795-4274
www.Xlibris.com
Orders@Xlibris.com
89123

Contents

Dedication

To my wonderful friends:
Sonja, Shearer, Sally, Bea, and Mary Sue

Also dedicated to my children:
Laura, David, Lynne, and Jenny,
who are always there to help

PREFACE

This book is done by request from family and friends. It is fiction (with the exception of Canoe), and its only purpose is to be funny. It is mostly a list of things that could happen, not things that did happen. I apologize to all the men I have dated in the last ten years if I have written anything that is offensive to you. I didn't mean to offend anyone. I also apologize to my lady friends for letting everyone know that we even talk about these things.

In case you haven't noticed, I must not have been very good on the dating scene. I really wanted a good man in my life and tried hard to find him. So whatever mistakes the men made, I did no better with my part of the date. I am just trying to hold on to my life and my sense of humor.

The book is arranged in chapters with each chapter having a quote, a list, a story and a picture. In addition there are two extra list of advice in general for older folks who want to date and a list of things people put in their profile for Match.com. Since most folks tend to exaggerate when they describe themselves, I have tried to explain some of the most often used words or phrases to help you figure out the truth.

I hope you enjoy the book.

GENERAL ADVICE

- Don't make long-range plans; life is too unpredictable.

- Do not ignore beeps from either person's pacemaker.

- If he offers you a peep at Little Molly, be sure he has a cat named Little Molly.

- If his Viagra does not seem to be functioning normally, drop him off at the nearest hospital and head for home.

- Brag on his dog or grandbaby, whether they bite you or not.

- Remember, prison guards do *not* wear striped uniforms with numbers.

- Ignore weird noises coming from your date as long as he seems alert.

- A gun on a date is a real deal breaker.

VOCABULARY

When learning about a potential date, there are several typical pieces of information you may want to gather. Whether online or over the telephone, here is a list of helpful definitions to help minimize surprises when and if you actually meet.

Dine in—you cook
Dine out—drive-through at a fast-food restaurant
Attends church regularly—every Easter
Long walks on beach—walks from car to beach
A little overweight—325 pounds
Plays golf—miniature
Full head of hair—several
Spiritual but not religious—warlock/witch
Sixties—sixty-nine and one half
Rich—good social security
Tall—five feet and three inches (with shoes)
Loves animals—deer hunter

Plays musical instrument—harmonica
Nice home—double-wide
Nice teeth—dentures
Slight limp—one legged
Brown hair—both of them
Good health—able to stand alone (for short periods)

CHAPTER ONE
A Typical Date

Quote

Delta Dawn, what's that flower you have on?
—Helen Reddy

Important List

What Not to Discuss on a Date:

- Former wife
- Cholesterol
- Flu shots
- Former wife
- Colonoscopies
- Arthritis
- Former wife

- Strokes
- Blood pressure
- Former wife

Story

Bless His Heart

Mary Jean had lost her husband to death almost a year ago and had not even thought about dating another man. Her cousin, Hilda, had tried and tried to interest Mary Jean in doing something to make her life more interesting and happy. When Sara Hendricks died, Hilda thought immediately of introducing Mary Jean to Sara's widowed husband, Herbert.

After much discussing and begging, Mary Jean agreed to meet Herbert in the big-city restaurant that had been erected just outside of town. Although he had never been there either, Herbert was excited that Mary Jean wanted to meet him and quickly agreed to the plan.

The plan was that they meet each other at the restaurant's door and introduce themselves. Herbert was to wear a pink carnation, and Mary Jean would carry white gloves so that they would recognize each other.

When Mary Jean pulled up to the restaurant alone, she was confused by the large number of cars and the unfamiliar music coming from inside. There were bright lights twinkling in front, and it seemed like a happy place where younger folks could come out for a night of good food and entertainment. She was already uneasy about being there and especially confused about meeting someone new. She was not sure if her medium-high heels and long skirt would fit in.

Bravely, Mary Jean gathered up her black bag, adjusted her skirt, and stepped out of the car. Locating Herbert was no problem at all. He was waiting for her near the front door. She could not miss the large pink carnation on the coat of his leisure suit, but the multicolored bow tie seemed to glare at her and at the hostess who offered to find a table for them.

His hair, what was left of it, was neatly combed sideways in an attempt to cover his large bald spot. The missing tooth hardly showed when he smiled at her. Bless his heart.

After a few awkward minutes, Mary Jean asked how he was doing and commented that the weather had been unusually warm for this time of year. He agreed and brought up the subject of his wife. "She was the sweetest thing God ever created," he volunteered. "We had fifty-six years of married bliss."

"I'm sure you did," Mary Jean replied as she picked up the menu. She asked what looked good to him. "I will never forget her," he continued.

"I'm sure you won't, and have you looked at the menu?" she asked again. After a few sad moments of contemplation, he inquired as to whether they might have tomato sandwiches on the menu. "My wife could fix a fine tomato sandwich," he remembered.

Mary Jean quickly decided she would order fried chicken and perhaps some potatoes and beans. Fortunately, Herbert agreed that it sounded good to him too. So the contents of the meal were decided.

In an effort to start a meaningful conversation, Mary Jean asked if Herbert had seen any good movies recently. She also asked who might be his favorite actor or actress. "My wife always enjoyed the picture show," he answered. "I think her favorite actor was John Wayne. I always preferred Betty Grable myself."

Thankfully, the chicken with the beans and potatoes arrived, and they could take a talking break to have their meal. It looked as if he was enjoying his food and might not think about his wife for a few minutes. Unfortunately, his first words after eating a bite were, "My wife sure could fry a good chicken."

It was a relief when Mary Jean and Herbert said their good-byes at the door before going to their own cars. "Bless his heart," she thought as she added another rule to her dating agenda—that is, if she ever wanted to try again. Rule number 5, don't talk about your ex-wife or ex-husband. She hoped that Herbert would expand his interests and vocabulary before another woman agreed to date him.

CHAPTER TWO
Finding Mr. Right

Quote

Take me out to the ball game.

Important List

Where to Meet:

- Church
- Bingo
- Internet
- Grocery store
- Bars and restaurants
- Taking long walks on the beach
  (Does anybody actually do that?)
- Ball games

Story

The Playing Field

When it comes to dating, the playing field for a seventy-year-old straight white female when compared with that of a much-younger person is very, very limited. I think the odds are seven women to one man. Most men don't acknowledge that fact as each of them firmly believes he is God's gift to the women of the world. It doesn't seem to matter if he is fat, old, feeble, and bald. Each one still thinks the women want him because of his good looks. It has been said that when a man loses his wife to death, women start bringing over casseroles as soon as they can after the funeral, without losing community respect. Chances are, they will be remarried within the year, probably to someone they have been friends with for a long time.

About a year ago, a man called Trudy to tell her that his wife had died recently. She reacted with mixed feelings. Since his wife and Trudy had been friends once, it brought a sense of sadness. She was sorry to hear of his wife's death. She was ashamed that it also brought a measure of hope in the fact that he had called and was now available.

This was a good Christian man. Trudy had known him and his family for many years and thought that he would make a good mate. He asked her to call him when she was in town as they were living about two hundred and fifty miles apart. She managed to find an excuse to go to her daughter's home, which was within easy commuting distance from this man. When she was there, she made a point to call him as soon as possible. She left a message on his machine.

When her visit neared its end and he had not called, Trudy called him again and found him ready to talk. He said that he had given some thought to the two of them getting together. He said he was sure it would have been a nice experience. He continued that he had prayed for a new person in his life since his wife had been gone for a few months. He prayed on a Tuesday night and went to church the following Wednesday night. While there, he happened to look to his side as he was going down the aisle, and lo and behold, there she stood.

This story provides an example of what the odds are for an older lady like me (or Trudy) getting there before the man is no longer available. It is a hopeless situation that older ladies find themselves in these days.

For those of us who are not fortunate enough to have a friend die and get a distinct advantage on the husband, we have to search for Mr. Right on our own. The question then is, "Where do we go to meet single men?" Church is always a good choice. In church, the ratio is much worse than in the world in general.

Recently, our church's token single man got married. His wife had died many years earlier, and the church ladies had been eyeing him for quite a while. He was tall, dark, and handsome even in his seventies. In addition to that, he was a really nice person and a Christian. There may be other single men in our church, but they seem to keep a low profile and slip out as unnoticed as possible.

For a few months, I secretly had my eye on a very decent man who was a regular attendee of prayer meetings. He was soft-spoken, friendly, and kind of cute. One day, he just disappeared. They say he left town without a good reason or destination. I sure hope he didn't hear about my crush on him.

While pondering the playing fields of meeting, I think of bingo. Both sexes seem to enjoy playing bingo. It doesn't take much energy, and everybody loves to win prizes. It is a good place to go on a Saturday night. If you are lucky, you might be served popcorn or hot dogs along with coffee or soft drinks. There is always a chance of finding that lone man who would honor you with his presence.

I have never been one to go to a bar, but I am a great patron of most restaurants. The bars sometimes have a place to dance, which gives a real opportunity to meet someone. Someday, if I live long enough, I am going to have to learn to dance.

Speaking of learning something that would help a woman to meet a man, golf would be a great game to learn. On the profiles for online dating services, most of the men say they like to play golf, and from personal experience, it seems that is true. It looks easy, and I really would love to be able to golf. It would be easier, though, if my right arm wasn't disabled due to an old shoulder injury.

The playing field is very small for single older women and rather large for single older men. At least, that is what we tell ourselves when we fail to find our Mr. Right.

CHAPTER THREE

Avoiding Misunderstandings

Quote

Lean on me.

Important List

What to Bring on a Date:

- Teeth
- Artificial limbs
- Hearing devices
- Umbrella
- Walking cane
- Glasses

- Epipen
- Important telephone/cell phone numbers
- Critical medications (such as Beano, Viagra)

Story

Oops!

When a person decides to meet a potential companion, he or she usually communicates by e-mail. Part of this correspondence includes sharing information about your appearance, your strengths, and your weaknesses.

Although most people build themselves up, some people are careful to warn others of imperfections in themselves—especially physical problems. Perhaps these people had rather someone be pleased when they meet rather than disappointed because of a potential problem. For example, a person may say that he or she is "a little overweight." This line works

best when the person is only a *little* overweight. Anything over three hundred pounds probably would not qualify.

I have always been careful to warn a man if I have anything that he might be disappointed in and have expected the same from him. There was a man that I will call Joe who did not understand the courtesy of warning his date of any potential problems. Joe and I agreed to meet at a steak house located between where he and I lived. We were to see each other, talk with each other during dinner, and find out if we had anything in common that might make us want to see each other again.

I arrived a few minutes before Joe and got out of my car so that it would be easy for him to find me. I glanced at each car as it came in, looking for an older man alone. A car soon pulled up near where I was standing. I couldn't help but notice that the man and woman in it were looking at me and smiling.

The woman who had been driving got out of the car first and then went to the passenger's side to help the man with his walker. They both smiled and came up to me. I whispered the name Joe, and he replied yes. He introduced the lady as his caretaker, and together, the three of us entered the restaurant. After we were seated, the caretaker explained that she would be back to get him in an hour and wished us a nice dinner.

Joe explained that he had had a severe stroke and that he was looking for someone who would be interested in marrying him and taking care of him. He said that he had a serious relationship with a lady he intended to marry before the stroke but that now she only wanted to be friends.

He also had one son who lived nearby and who would one day inherit everything that Joe owned.

We had a pleasant meal, and the hour passed quickly. When the caretaker returned, I politely thanked Joe for the meal and for the opportunity to meet him.

When I got to my car, it would not crank. As I tried and tried to start the car, I glanced out of my side window and saw Joe and his caretaker backing out of their spot and heading to the highway. As much as I hated to see them go, I knew that neither of them would be able to help, and there was no need to embarrass him.

A few minutes later, the car started and ran for about one-fourth of a mile. It went far enough to get me into real trouble. I was in the lane to get onto the expressway and three lanes over from the curb when the engine stopped for good. Cars zoomed all around me, and there was zero chance of my getting anywhere on my own. I did the only things I knew to do: I prayed and dialed 911. Because of the situation and the location, 911 could not help, but I think the prayer did.

As I sat there in utter frustration, I saw a pickup truck backing up to the front of my disabled car. The driver of the truck, a very nice young black man, simply asked if I would like some help. That must have been the understatement of the year as I was so desperate for his help. He went back to his truck and came back with a strong rope that he attached to both his truck and my car.

He got back into his truck and pointed his hand over the cab of the truck to let other drivers understand and to stop for the truck to pull my car over to the curb and into a nearby station. When we both got out, I was thanking him over and over. He gave me a nice hug and offered to stay with me until someone could come to help.

The kindness of a young black man to an old white lady will never be forgotten.

You Can't Be Too Careful

Quote

Waiting is the hardest part.

Important List

What Not to Bring on a Date:

- Try not to bring obvious medical apparatus unless absolutely necessary (for example, an oxygen tank or a wheelchair)
- Gun (or other weapons)
- Nude photos of self or others
- Pictures of former wife or husband

- Caretaker
- Wedding rings
- Recent lab results/medical reports
- Son-in-law

Story

Ralph

Ralph is Sara Beth's son-in-law. He is very patient with her when she spends time with his wife, who is her daughter. Since they live in Atlanta, it is sometimes easier to get together with men in the city than where Sara Beth lives in the country. Ralph surely never wanted to get involved in her dating experiences, but as a favor to his wife, one time he did.

Tim and Sara Beth had gotten acquainted through an Internet dating service and, of course, wanted to meet each other. They were both familiar with a cafeteria near where Ralph and Lynne lived. They decided it would be the ideal place to meet.

Lynne was not pleased with her mother meeting strange men, even in a safe environment. She only agreed to the date if Ralph would go along as a secret chaperone. By secret, Lynne meant that Sara Beth would see Ralph and know he was there, but Tim would have no idea he was being watched. In case things did not go well or Sara Beth needed a ride home, she was pleased to know help was available.

Tim and Sara Beth met out in front of the cafeteria. They had no trouble finding each other. They struck up a conversation quickly. They continued to talk all through the meal as they sat facing each other at the small table. Sarah Beth did think to glance around for Ralph, but he was nowhere to be seen. She assumed he had decided not to come or maybe thought she and Tim were okay and left. She remembered to look for him from time to time as she enjoyed the conversation with Tim. They actually had a lot in common and spent nearly two hours conversing.

By the time they left to go to the parking lot, it was late, quiet, and dark. Few cars were left in the parking lot, when she was astonished to see Ralph. He was waiting outside the whole time. Needless to say, he was cold and bored.

Sara Beth could not apologize enough. Now that is what she would call a good son-in-law. She never thought of him waiting outside and was ashamed that she had stayed so long. The misunderstanding and Ralph's sacrifice paid off because Tim and Sara Beth agreed for him to come down to spend the weekend with her family soon.

CHAPTER FIVE
Plan Ahead

Quote

I want to go home, I want to go home, oh, Lord, I want to go home.

Important List

Places Not to Go on a Date:

- Political rally
- Former wife's grave
- Former husband's grave
- Forest for deer hunting
- Skating rink
- Theaters that play X-rated movies

- Motel
- Mass-merchandising store

Story

A Date for Clyde

This was a setup and not a good one for either of them. Nora's beautician, Sue, thought she needed to meet a nice man who had recently lost his wife. He was so lonely and spent many hours with the ladies at the beauty shop. Sue assured Nora that he was a nice man and would do her no harm. Sue said he just needed someone to talk to and be his friend.

It is always a good idea to plan the details of a date over the telephone. Where you will go on a date and at least some idea of what to do should be planned ahead. Unfortunately, most dates between older men and women at least start out at a place to eat. It is just sort of understood unless some other specific activity is planned in advance. Since Nora had not talked with her date or made plans, she assumed they would go out for dinner. She was expecting to have a nice conversation over a nice meal and get to know each other.

When Clyde arrived, he drove up in his new red truck and blew the horn (not off to a good start). After Nora climbed into the truck and introduced herself, she attempted a conversation. She began by asking, "Where will we go to eat?" "Oh," he replied, "I already ate at home." "Then what would you like to do?" Nora asked.

He suggested that she might like to drive his new truck. It was a sweet offer, so Nora tried to contain her excitement while she took over the driving. After riding around for a while, she drove to a local sandwich shop. They went in, and Nora bought herself a six-inch sandwich and a soft drink. Clyde had a soft drink. They sat in a booth and talked about his wife. Now that she thinks about it, talking about his wife was not that bad. He had had a long loving marriage and he missed her. It wasn't his fault that Nora was bitter because she had recently lost her husband of thirty-four years to a younger woman.

After the meal, neither of them could think of anything else to do, so Nora conveniently remembered that she had promised to babysit her granddaughter later that night. She pleaded that maybe they should make a short night of it. Nora drove back home and thanked him for a nice night. She let him walk her to the door. Clyde was a nice man, and Nora has no ill will toward him. However, she is still mad at the beautician who set them up.

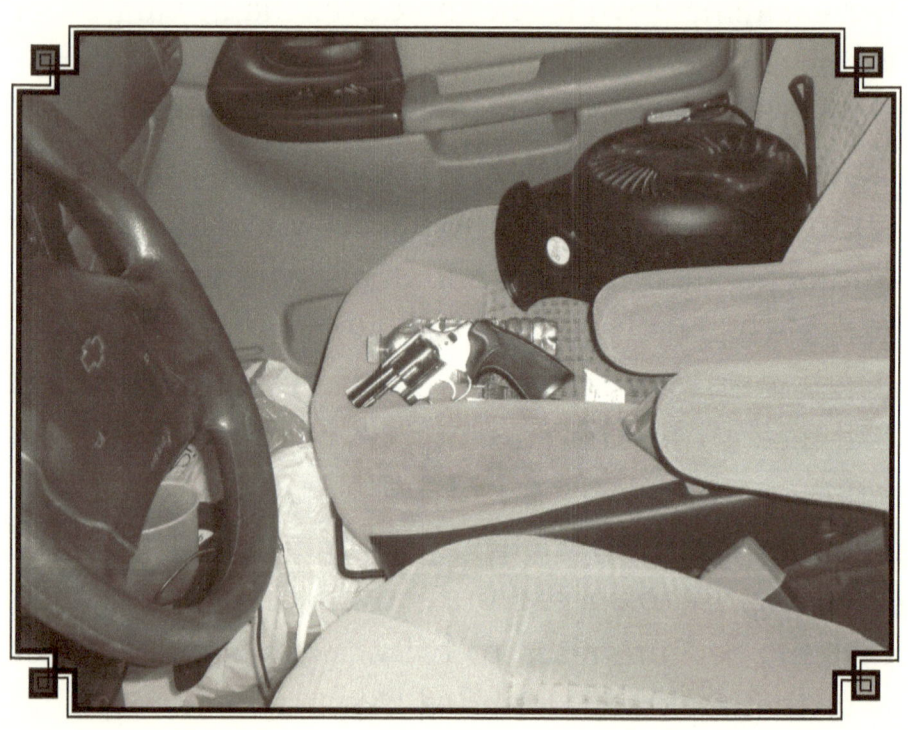

CHAPTER SIX

Beware of Stranger

Quote

Poor boy, you're bound to die.

Important List

Dangerous Items on a Date:

- Gun
- Knife
- Pills
- Car
- Animals
- Cane or pocketbook

Story

Thank God for Sally

Roy and I had talked several times on the telephone, but we lived in different states. There was not much hope for us to meet. He lived in North Carolina and I lived in South Georgia. He sounded like a really nice man. According to him, he had done a good job of raising several children and was also part of an up-and-coming musical group. He claimed to be a good Christian and talked a good talk.

It happened that my favorite cousin on my mother's side lives in Columbia, South Carolina. This was about halfway between our two homes. My friend and I had visited her several times, and it was time for another visit. It made sense that if Roy was willing to drive over a hundred miles to meet me, I could at least try to make time for him while we were visiting. Thank God my friend Sally would be going with me.

When we got off the expressway, there was an abandoned service station near the exit. It looked like a moderately safe place to meet. So after Sally and I left my cousin's, we called Roy on the cell phone. I asked if he would like to meet at the abandoned service station. He was already in the city, and it was easy for him to find the meeting place.

Roy was driving an old reddish van. There was so much clutter that we had to clean out a place to sit. We had agreed to go with him to a nearby place where we could talk and eat. I quickly debated whether to get in the van or not. I definitely would not have gotten in if I had been alone. Thank God for Sally. However, even with Sally's presence, my heart took a little jump and my hand gave a little shake when I saw the gun. It was lying open in the seat between us. This was something new, and it was too late to turn around and escape out the door.

I asked Roy about the gun, and he said it was just for protection and shifted it under his seat. We picked out the nearest place to eat and ordered barbecue and hamburgers. Roy took one bite of his barbecue and was still talking when Sally and I finished our lunch. I'm not sure if he ever took a second bite. He was an authority on any subject, including religion and politics. He talked not only to Sally and me but included the waitress too. He even talked to other folks seated nearby. Other than being a little overpowering and boring, his talk was not out of line, so we tried to relax. We were hoping that, eventually, he would finish his barbecue.

Roy's hair was down to his waist in length and was wound up in a knot at the back of his head. He was overweight, and his clothes were incredibly wrinkled from the long ride. He didn't seem to notice that my appearance, I'm sure, had left much to be desired too. "The long hair," he explained, "was for the Locks of Love Organization." This organization is for children who would need wigs after losing their hair due to cancer treatments. My opinion of Roy came up several notches when I heard this. It raised a few more notches when we were safely back in our car.

Today, Sally and I have a laugh and remember him as a nice older man. Although he was eccentric, he was just looking for new friends to share his music and his life.

CHAPTER SEVEN

He Marches to a Different Drummer

Quote

Row, row, row your boat.

Important List

Canoe's Special List:

- Beef jerky
- Canoe
- Paddle
- Sleeping bag
- Lantern
- Change of clothes

Story

Canoe

This is a true story, but you may not believe it. Canoe and I met through some kind of personal ad back in the late 1990s. His real name is Gene Bennett, but he only goes by Canoe. He lives on the rivers of the United States. His home is a tent or a blanket, and he sleeps wherever he lands each day.

Canoe is half Native American and half European. He grew up on the Iroquois Indian Reservation in upstate New York. It was a hard life, where he was abused by his father and neglected by his mother. He learned the Indian ways, including how to live off the land.

When Gene turned eighteen, the Vietnam War was in full swing, and he gladly joined the U.S. Army. His primary goal was to escape from his deplorable home life. It was a difficult, unhappy time for him. In addition to the life of fighting for his country, he became involved with a native girl. He fell very much in love with this young girl. It was an awful mistake as she became pregnant and delivered a baby girl. He was adamant that the girl and the baby were killed for their involvement with an American. I am not sure that I believe that part of his story.

After several years of fighting the unpopular war in Vietnam, Gene arrived home. He was with a plane full of fellow soldiers that landed at an airport filled with war protesters. Instead of being the heroes they thought they were, they were called traitors. In disgust, Gene went to the hardware store and used his severance pay to buy a canoe and camping supplies. He went to the nearest river and made his home there for many years. He lived alone and slept on the ground in his tent. He communicated with no one except nature and stopped only to pick up his check and buy supplies.

At the time we met, Gene had tried to come off the river and settle down. He found a cabin to live in and a job in a sawmill. We met though an ad and corresponded for several months before he decided to come to Georgia to meet me. By this time, he had acquired an old truck. It took a lot of prayer for the old thing to hold up for the trip.

He spent a few days with my family and me. At night, he stayed in my mobile home alone while I slept next door with my family. He said he couldn't sleep on the soft bed, so he slept on the floor. He enjoyed the food that my daughter and I cooked. He said that it had been years since he had eaten such delicious meals. We are not really very good cooks.

I learned a great deal during Canoe's visit. He shared his experiences from living on the river with me. The most interesting experience that he shared was camping out on a deserted island. This island was completely deserted, and no human had ever lived there. Canoe said a well-known legend involved a lady ghost that haunted the island. Canoe swore that he had visited and talked with her there.

Canoe also shared that he went from place to place always on the river in the canoe. He was a legend in his own time as he would stop at the villages along the way. Sometimes, he would stay for a night or even a few days. He would return to some of the villages from time to time. The children were always excited to see him and hear of his adventures. The children of those villages were the ones who gave him the name Canoe.

Eventually, he decided to attempt to settle down and chose one of those villages for his new home. This village was one where the people had embraced him and enjoyed his stories.

Canoe was a walking science or history book. He learned about the earth from living a different way. After his short visit and a good-bye hug, he went back up north to his cabin and his job. Sadly, he wrote later that when he arrived home, all of his possessions, though few, had been stolen. This despicable act again destroyed his faith in human beings. Soon after his return, his last letter told me that he was going back to the river. As far as I know, he is still there living in his tent and traveling in his canoe.

Conclusion

On a More Serious Note

It is always good to have fun and laugh together when something is funny. I hope this book has given you a good laugh. Additionally, I pray that no one was offended by any of it. If you were, I sincerely apologize. It sometimes hurts to get old both physically and mentally. Oftentimes, we have to laugh to keep from crying. I hope you will experience more times of laughter than sadness.

Even though I have had no real success in the dating world, I am still hoping that God will send someone for me to love. When I have been away for a few hours or a few days, it would be wonderful to have someone meet me at the door and say, "Welcome home." Sometimes, just knowing another heart is beating in the house is a comfort and pushes the loneliness away.

I miss having a shoulder to cry on or having someone to take my side even when I am wrong. Cooking would not be such a chore if there was someone to cook for. Eating alone is hard whether at home or eating out. It would be great to have someone to sit with in church. Perhaps even feel a strong arm around my shoulders. We could be happy at night when we share prayers for both of our children. It would be nice to know there was no empty space on the other side of the bed. Everyone needs a traveling companion, and there are times when a good lady friend just doesn't quite meet the need.

My experiences with men and with dating will continue to accumulate and hopefully culminate in a wonderful relationship. I will keep my eyes open and my smile on for a new Mr. Right. I hope to someday go into a restaurant and gaze into the eyes of a wonderful man and proudly say, "Table for two."

AFTERTHOUGHT

If you talk, I'll listen
If you hurt, I'll comfort
If you call, I'll answer
If you're sick, I'll take care of you
If you're happy, I'll laugh with you
If you have children, I'll love them if they let me
And I will share my children with you.

Other Books by the Author:

While the Coffee Perks
Let God be the Judge

www.ingramcontent.com/pod-product-compliance
Lightning Source LLC
Chambersburg PA
CBHW050336290526
45785CB00006B/2516